PUBLISHIG HOUSE

KULTURE KITCHEN

POWER XL

AIR FRYER GRILL

COOKBOOK

The Cookbook Series That Will Help You To Conquer Your New Favorite Kitchen Appliance!

Snack & Sandwich Vol.2

PUBLISHIG HOUSE

POWER XL
AIR FRYER GRILL
COOKBOOK

EVERYDAY QUICK & EASY RECIPES FOR AIR FRYER LOVERS

Table of Content

INTRODUCTION 7

SNACK & SANDWICH 9

SMOKED SAUSAGE MIX 11
MUSHROOM OATMEAL 13
CAULIFLOWER AVOCADO TOAST 15
GARLIC AND CHEESE BREAD ROLLS 17
WHEAT andSEED BREAD 19
DINNER ROLLS 21
ROASTED BELL PEPPER ROLLS 23
STUFFED PEPPERS 25
CREAMY CAULIFLOWER AND HAM BLEND 27
SPICY THAI BITES 29
ROLLED FLANKS 31
VEAL CLUB SANDWICH 33
EGGPLANT SANDWICH 35
SHRIMP SANDWICHES 37
MOZZARELLA SPINACH ROLLS 39
CRISPY EGGPLANT STRIPS 41
CRISP PARMESAN-POTATO BALLS 43
SWEET POTATO AND PARSNIPS CRISPS 45
POTATOES AU GRATIN 47
AIR FRIED KALE CHIPS 49
AIR-FRIED CALAMARI 51
CHEDDAR BACON CROQUETTES 53
MOROCCAN MEATBALLS WITH MINT YOGURT 55
TOMATO, CHEESE 'N BROCCOLI QUICHE 57
TASTY HASH BROWN 59
PORK BARBECUE SANDWICH 61
FISH CLUB SANDWICH 63
AIR FRYER SANDWICH 65
CHEESE SANDWICH 67
ONION FLOWERS 69
SWEET PEPPER AND POTATO STUFFED BREAD ROLLS 71
CRISPY PARSLEY AND GARLIC MUSHROOMS 73
CRISPY BROCCOLI TOTS 75
ROASTED WINTER VEGETABLES 77
CHEESY POLENTA 79
CAJUN SHRIMP 81
BROCCOLI ROUNDS WITH CHEESE 83
COCONUT CHICKEN BITES 85

Cauliflower Snack   87
Sausage Balls   89
Chicken Dip   91
Sweet Popcorn   93
Squash Fritters   95
Cauliflower Buffalo   97
Fries Avocado   99
Coco Milk and Paprika Drumstick   101

Introduction

 Elsie Tyler is a passionate cookbook writer with over a decade of culinary expertise. Known for her culinary skills and high standard, she has combined her classic recipes tailored to use with the modern cooking appliance in her new cookbook series "The Complete Power XL Air Fryer Grill Cookbook" Kulture Kitchen Publishing House. She loves to employ innovations in cooking by keeping the traditional elements and richness.

We can always find the art of simplicity in her recipes, making her a step ahead of many innovative cooking methods. All of her books include self-tested recipes, and the pleasure of sharing exciting experiments is evident in most of her recipe works.
Popularly known as a 'wizard of recipe developer' among her circle, she contributes recipes to several reputed magazines. She helps you discover something new and impressive. Beyond her books, she maintains a strong influence among her friends and family as an enthusiast of healthy eating and living.

Having spent considerable time writing the series "The Complete Power XL Air Fryer Grill Cookbook", she has carefully penned her research with super versatile meal ideas without compromising quality and nutritional values. Her approach to modern food tech is mind-blowing.
This Cookbook Series is a pioneering endeavor blended with modern cooking with traditional values by focusing on healthy, balanced food. It is a reference series for people who love having healthy food.

Snack & Sandwich

Smoked Sausage Mix

Ready in about 40 mins | Serving 4 | Easy

Ingredients:

- 1 and ½ pounds of smoked sausage, chopped and browned
- A pinch of salt and black pepper
- 1 and ½ cups of grits
- 4 and ½ cups of water
- 16 ounces of cheddar cheese, shredded
- 1 cup of milk
- ¼ teaspoon of garlic powder
- 1 and ½ teaspoons of thyme, chopped
- Cooking spray
- 4 eggs, whisked

Directions:

1. Put the water in a kettle, over medium heat, bring to a boil, add grits, stir, cover, simmer for 5 minutes and take off the heat.

2. Remove the cheese, whisk until it melts, then blend well with the butter, thyme, salt, pepper, garlic powder, and eggs.

3. Warm up the Power XL Air Fryer at 300° F, steam spray with grease, and add pork sausage.

4. Stir in grits, scatter and simmer for 25 minutes.

5. Serve for breakfast and split between dishes.

Enjoy!

Mushroom Oatmeal

Ready in about 30 min | Servings 4 | Normal

Ingredients:

- 1 small yellow onion, chopped
- 1 cup of steel-cut oats
- 2 garlic cloves, minced
- 2 tablespoons of butter
- ½ cup of water
- 14 ounces of canned chicken stock
- 3 thyme springs, chopped
- 2 tablespoons of extra virgin olive oil
- ½ cup of gouda cheese, grated
- 8 ounces of mushroom, sliced
- Salt and black pepper to the taste

Directions:

1. Heat a pan over medium heat that suits your Power XL Air Fryer with the butter, add onions and garlic, stir and cook for 4 minutes.

2. Attach oats, sugar, salt, pepper, stock, and thyme, stir, place in the Air Fryer and cook for 16 minutes at 360° F.

3. In the meantime, prepare a skillet over medium heat with the olive oil, add mushrooms, cook them for 3 minutes, add oatmeal and cheese, whisk, divide into bowls and serve for breakfast.

Enjoy!

Cauliflower Avocado Toast

Ready in about 23 min | Servings 2 | Normal

Ingredients:

- 1 (12-ounce) steamer bag cauliflower

- 1 large egg

- 1/2 cup of shredded mozzarella cheese

- 1 ripe medium avocado

- 1/2 teaspoon of garlic powder

- 1/4 teaspoon of ground black pepper

Directions:

1. Whisk the eggs and the cream together in a medium bowl. Pour into a round baking dish with 4 cups.

2. Apply and combine the cauliflower, then finish with Cheddar. Drop the dish into the tray for the Power XL Air Fryer.

3. Set the temperature to 320° F and change the timer for 20 minutes.

4. When fully cooked, the eggs are firm, and the cheese is browned. Cut into 4 bits.

5. Dice the avocado and uniformly break into bits. Using 2 tablespoons of sour cream, sliced scallions, and crumbled bacon to cover each portion. Enjoy!

Garlic and Cheese Bread Rolls

Ready in about 15 min | Servings 2 | Normal

Ingredients:

8 tablespoons of grated cheese

6 teaspoons of melted butter

Garlic bread spice mix

2 bread rolls

Directions:

1. Slice the bread rolls from the top in a crisscross pattern butnot cut through at the bottom.

2. Put all the cheese into the slits and brush the tops of the bread rolls with melted butter. Sprinkle the garlic mix on the rolls.

3. Select bake mode the set the temperature to heat the Power XL Air Fryer to 350° F. Place the rolls into the basket and cook untilcheese is melted for about 5 minutes.

4. When the timer reaches 0, then press the cancel button

Enjoy!

Wheat andSeed Bread

Ready in about 1 hour 28 min | Servings 4 | Normal

Ingredients:

- 3½ ounces of flour
- 1 teaspoon of yeast
- 1 teaspoon of salt
- 3½ ounces of wheat flour
- ¼ cup of pumpkin seeds

Directions:

1. Mix the wheat flour, yeast, salt, seeds, and plain flour in a large bowl. Stir in ¾ cup of lukewarm water, and keep stirring until dough becomes soft.

2. Knead for another 5 minutes until the dough becomes elastic and smooth. Mold into a ball and cover with a plastic bag. Set aside for 30 minutes for it to rise.

3. Select bake mode the set the temperature to heat your Power XL Air Fryer to 392° F.

4. Transfer the dough into a small pizza pan and place it in the Air Fryer. Bake for 18 minutes until golden. Remove and place on a wire rack to cool. Enjoy!

Dinner Rolls

Ready in about 22 min | Servings 4 | Easy

Ingredients:

- 1 cup of shredded mozzarella cheese
- 1 ounce of full-Fat: cream cheese
- 1 cup of blanched finely ground almond flour
- 1/4 cup of ground flaxseed
- ½ teaspoon of baking powder
- 1 large egg

Directions:

1. In a large microwave-safe dish, put the mozzarella, cream cheese, and almond flour—1-minute Microwave. Mix until smooth.

2. Substitute the flaxseed, baking powder, and egg until smooth and fully mixed. If it gets too rigid, pulse another 15 seconds.

3. Set the dough apart into six pieces and roll it into balls. Place the balls in the basket for Power XL Air Fryer.

4. Switch to 320° F and set the timer for 12 minutes.

5. Cause the rolls to thoroughly cool before serving.

Roasted Bell Pepper Rolls

Ready in about 20 min | Servings 6 | Normal

Ingredients:

- 1 yellow bell pepper, halved
- 1 orange bell pepper, halved
- Salt and black pepper to the taste
- 4 ounces of feta cheese, crumbled
- 1 green onion, chopped
- 2 tablespoons of oregano, chopped

Directions:

1. Mix the cheese and the onion, oregano, salt, and pepper in a cup and whisk well.

2. Place halves of bell pepper in the basket of your Power XL Air Fryer, cook for 10 minutes at 400° F, move to a cutting board, cool down, and peel.

3. When the timer reaches 0, then press the cancel button

4. Break the cheese mixture into each half of the bell pepper, slice, secure with toothpicks, place on a plate, and serve as an appetizer.

Enjoy!

Stuffed Peppers

Ready in about 18 min | Servings 8 | Normal

Ingredients:

- 8 small bell peppers, tops cut off and seeds removed
- 1 tablespoon of olive oil
- Salt and black pepper to the taste
- 3.5 ounces of goat cheese, cut into 8 pieces

Directions:

1. In a cup, add salt and pepper to the cheese and oil, and mix to cover.

2. Fill each pepper with goat cheese, put them in the basket of your Power XL Air Fryer, cook for 8 minutes at 400° F, arrange them on a platter and serve as an appetizer.

Enjoy!

Creamy Cauliflower and Ham Blend

Ready in about 2hr 10 min | Servings 6 | Difficult

Ingredients:

- 8 grated ounces of cheddar cheese
- 4 ounces of ham, cubed cups
- 14 ounces of chicken
- 1/2 tablespoon of crushed garlic
- 1/2 tablespoon of ground onion
- Salt and black pepper, to satisfy
- 4 cloves of garlic, diced
- 1/4 cup of milk
- 16 ounces of cauliflower blossoms

Directions:

1.Blend ham and stock cheese in a pot that suits your Power XL Air Fryer. Mix cauliflower, powdered garlic, onion powder, milk, chili pepper, lime and stir in heavy cream, put the fryer in the air, and cook 300° F for 30minutes.

2. When the timer reaches 0, then press the cancel button

3. Split in and place in pots.

Enjoy!

Spicy Thai Bites

Ready in about 20 min | Servings 4 | Normal

Ingredients:

- 400 g of minced pork
- 1 sizeable onion
- 1 tablespoon of garlic puree
- 1 tablespoon of soy sauce
- 1 tablespoons of Worcestersauce
- 1 tablespoon of Thai red curry pasta
- 1/2 (rind and juice) lime
- 1 tablespoon of blended spice
- 1 tablespoon ofChinese spice
- 1 tablespoon of coriander
- Salt and pepper

Directions:

1. In a tub, put all the ingredients and blend well.

2. Put them in the Power XL Air Fryer and form them into balls.

3. Cook for 15 minutes at a heat of 365° F in the Air Fryer.

4. When setting a cooking time less than 20 minutes, first set the cooking time to 20 minutes.

Then, turn the time/darkness control knob to the desired cooking time

5 Enjoy

Rolled Flanks

Ready in about 30 min | Servings 4 | Normal

Ingredients:

- 1 8-ounce of crescent rolls can
- 1 12-ounce of package cocktail franks

Directions:

1. Drain the cocktail franks and pat dry on paper towels. Cut the dough into rectangular-shaped strips, about 1-inch x 1.5-inch.

2. Roll the cut strips around the franks, ensuring that the ends can be seen. Make them firm by placing them in the freezer for 5 minutes.

3. Preheat the Power XL Air Fryer to 330° F. Take the franks out from the freezer and place it in the cooking basket—Cook for 6 to8 minutes.

4. Reset the temperature to 390ºF and cook again for 3 minutes. Once it is golden brown, remove, serve, and enjoy.

Veal Club Sandwich

Ready in about 30 min | Servings 4 | Normal

Ingredients:

- Two slices of whole white bread
- 1 tablespoons of smooth butter
- 1/2 pounds of cubed veal
- 1 small capsicum

For barbeque sauce:

- 1/4 tablespoons Worcestershire
- 1/2 crushed garlic flake
- 1/4 cup of ointment
- 1/4 tablespoons powder mustard
- 1/2 tablespoons sugar
- 1/4 tablespoons hot sauce with chili
- 1 1/2 cup of water

Directions:

1. Take the bread slices and cut the rims. Now horizontally cut the slices.

2. Heat the sauce ingredients and wait before sauce thickens. Now bring in the veal to the sauce until the flavors are obtained—roast in the capsicum and peel off the skin. The capsicum is sliced into strips. Combine products, and apply it to slices of bread.

3. Select bake mode the set the temperature to preheat the Power XL Air Fryer to 300° F for five minutes. Open the Fryer basket and put the sandwiches prepared in it so that no two Sandwiches bump into each other.

4. Now keep the fryer at 250° F for Fifteen minutes. Switch the sandwiches in-between the cooking process both slices. Serve the sandwiches with spicy ketchup or mint chutney.

Eggplant Sandwich

Ingredients

- Bread of preference
- 1 small Eggplants, halved and sliced
- 1 tablespoons olive oil
- 2 French sandwinch rolls
- 1\2 cup crumbled feta cheese
- Aioli or other sauce to taste
- Parsley cut

Directions:

Preheat your oven's broiler.

Cut the eggplants into cubes. In the mold of the Power XL Air Fryer place, the eggplants varnished with olive oil.

Spread a sheet of bread with the aioli and add the eggplants.

Add the olive oil with the parsley in another layer.

Close the sandwich and Serve up.

Shrimp Sandwiches

Ready in about 15 min | Servings 4 | Easy

Ingredients:

- 1 and ¼ cups of cheddar, shredded
- 6 ounces of canned tiny shrimp, drained
- 3 tablespoons of mayonnaise
- 2 tablespoons of green onions, chopped
- 4 whole-wheat bread slices
- 2 tablespoons of butter, soft

Directions:

1. Mix shrimp and cheese, green onion, and mayo in a cup, then mix well.

2. Place this over half of the slices of bread, cover with the other slices of bread, diagonally split into halves, and sprinkle butter over them.

3. Place the sandwiches in the Power XL Air Fryer and cook for 5 minutes at 350° F.

4. When the timer reaches 0, then press the cancel button

5. Split shrimp on sandwiches and serve for breakfast.

Enjoy!

Mozzarella Spinach Rolls

Ready in about 25 min | Servings 2 | Normal

Ingredients:

- 10½ ounces of spinach leaves, boiled
- 1 tablespoon of grated mozzarella cheese
- 2 tablespoons of breadcrumbs
- 1 onion, finely chopped
- 1clove of garlic, grated
- 1 tablespoon of vegetable oil
- 1 teaspoon of ground red chili
- Salt to taste
- 2 tablespoons of corn flour

Directions:

1. Mash the spinach to make a puree;add the mozzarella, breadcrumbs, garlic, corn flour, and salt. Mix thoroughly and mold into small balls.

2. Mix the onions and red chili with some cheese and mold them into smallerballs. Make a hole into the spinach rolls and insert the cheese rolls into each one. Ensure the rolls are evenly covered on all sides.

3. Brush the rolls with oil and place them in an Power XL Air Fryer at 390° F. Cook for about15 minutes until crisp, and serve with a tomato sauce.

Crispy Eggplant Strips

Ready in about 30 min | Servings 2 | Normal

Ingredients:

- 4 tablespoons of cornstarch
- 1 medium-sized eggplant
- 4 tablespoons of vegetable oil
- 1 pinch of salt
- 4 tablespoons of water

Directions:

1. Select bake mode the set the temperature to heat your Power XL Air Fryer to 390°F.

2. Slice the eggplant into 0.3 x 3 inches strips.

3. Mix the oil, cornstarch, and water in a bowl. Add the eggplant strips and mix to coat evenly.

4. Put half of the eggplant strips in the Air Fryer and cook for about 14 minutes until they begin to brown. Do the same to the next batch of eggplant strips until they are all cooked.

5. Serve while hot with a yogurt dip.

Crisp Parmesan-Potato Balls

Ready in about25 min | Servings 4 | Normal

Ingredients:

For the Filling:

- 8 ounces of Parmesan, grated
- 2 egg yolks
- 6 teaspoons of flour
- A pinch of nutmeg
- 4 medium-sized potatoes, peeled and chopped
- 1½ ounce of chopped chives
- A pinch of ground black pepper
- A pinch of salt

For the Breading:

- 6 ounces of breadcrumbs
- 6 ounces of flour
- 2 eggs, whisked
- 3 tablespoons of olive oil

Directions:

1. Cook the potatoes in water with a little salt for about 15 minutes and drain.

2. Use a potato masher to mash the potatoes to form a pulped mass and allow it tocool.

3. Add the parmesan, egg yolk, chives, and flour and mix thoroughly. Addthe salt, nutmeg, and pepper. Roll the potato fillings into small round balls.

4. Select bake mode the set the temperature to heat your Power XL Air Fryer to 390°F.

5. Add the oil to the breadcrumbs and mix with finger tips until it become scrumbly.

6. Roll the balls over the flour, dip into the whisked eggs, and lastly, coat with the breadcrumbs. Press to ensure coating sticks firmly.

7. Put the potato balls into the basket and Air Fry until golden for about 8 minutes.

Enjoy!

Sweet Potato and Parsnips Crisps

Ready in about 25 min | Servings 2 | Normal

Ingredients:

- 1 medium-sized sweet potato, peeled
- 2 medium-sized beets
- 2 medium-sized parsnips
- ½ teaspoon of ground chili
- 3 teaspoons of vegetable oil

Directions:

1. Select bake mode the set the temperature to preheat your Power XL Air Fryer to 460° F.

2. Cut the beets, potato, and parsnips into thin slices. Add the oil, chili, salt, and pepper, and then toss to mix.

3. Put into Air Fryer and cook for 10 minutes. Shake the pan and continue cooking until crisp and golden for another 10 minutes.

Potatoes Au Gratin

Ready in about 45 min | Servings 6 | Normal

Ingredients:

- 7 medium russet potatoes, peeled and sliced wafer-thin
- ½ cup of cream
- ½ cup of milk
- 1 teaspoon of black pepper
- ½ teaspoon of nutmeg
- ½ cup of gruyere, grated

Directions:

1. Select bake mode the set the temperature to preheat the Power XL Air Fryer to 390° F. Combine cream and milk in a bowland then season with nutmeg, pepper, and salt to taste.

2. Coat the thinly sliced potato with the milk mixture and then remove it to abaking dish.

3. Pour the remaining cream mixture on top of the potatoes. Put the baking dish in the cooking basket into the Air Fryer. Cook for 25 minutes and then remove it.

4. Distribute the cheese uniformly over the potatoes. Bake for 10 minutes until brown.

Air fried Kale Chips

Ready in about 9 min | Servings 1-2 | Normal

Ingredients:

- 1 head of kale

- 1 tablespoon of olive oil

- 1 teaspoon of soyasauce

Directions:

1. Take out the center steam of the kale and tear it up into1 1/2 pieces. Wash the pieces and dry well.

2. Next, toss with the soya sauce and olive oil. Place in the Power XL Air Fryer at 400° F for 2 to 3 minutes, tossing halfway through. Enjoy!

Air-Fried Calamari

Ready in about 20 min | Servings 2 | Normal

Ingredients:

- 1 1/2 pounds of baby squid, cut hoods into rings, and separate tentacles.
- 5-6 cups + 2 tablespoons of vegetable oil
- 1/2 cup of semolina flour
- 1/2 cup of all-purpose flour
- 1/2 teaspoon of old Bay seasoning
- 1/3 cup of plain cornmeal
- ½ teaspoon of black salt pepper, to the taste

Directions:

1. Rinse squid well in cold water. Cut off the tentacles using one cut but keep1/4 an inch of the hood to keep all the tentacles in one piece. For larger squid, make them bite-sized by cutting pieces in half lengthwise.

2. Add oil to a medium-sized deep pot; the oil must reach 4 inches up the side ofthe pot. Heat the oil to 325°F. In the meantime, combine the dry mixture in a

bowl and set aside.

3. With the oil heated up, dredge your squid. Squeeze off any liquid and dredge the squid in the dry mixture. (Work in batches).

4. Lower the calamari gently into the hot oil and fry back and forth. Remove after 2 to 1/2 minutes or golden brown. Drain on a paper-towel-lined plate (work in batches).

5. Serve with marinara sauce and lemon wedges on the side.

Cheddar Bacon Croquettes

Ready in about 50 min | Servings 4 | Normal

Ingredients:

For the Filling:

- 1-poundof bacon, sliced thinly and set at room temperature
- 1-poundof sharp cheddar cheese, block (cut into 6 portions of 1-inch x 1¾-inch each)

For the Breading:

- 1 cup of all-purpose flour
- 4 tablespoons of olive oil
- 1 cup of seasoned breadcrumbs

Directions:

1. Wrap 2 bacon pieces around each cheddar piece completely. Trim off any fat excess, freeze the cheddar bacon bites for 5 minutes to make firm, but not to freeze.

2. Preheat Power XL Air Fryer to 390° F. Combine the breadcrumbs and oil and stir untilit becomes loose and crumbly.

3. Put the cheddar block into the flour, place the eggs, and then finally the breadcrumbs, pressing the coating to the croquettes to make sure it sticks.

4. To prevent cheese from running out, double the coating by dipping twice into the egg and then the breadcrumbs

5. Place the croquettes in the basket and cook until golden brown or for about 8 minutes.

Moroccan Meatballs with Mint Yogurt

Ready in about 35 min | Servings 4 | Normal

Ingredients:

For the Meatballs

- 1 egg white
- 4 ounces of ground turkey
- 1-poundof ground lamb
- 1 tablespoon of mint, finely chopped
- 1½ tablespoons of parsley, finely chopped
- 1teaspoon of ground cumin
- 1 teaspoon of cayenne pepper
- 1 teaspoon of ground coriander
- 1 teaspoon of red chili paste
- ¼ cup of olive oil
- 2 garlic cloves, finely chopped
- 1 teaspoon of salt

For the Mint Yogurt:

- ¼ cup of sour cream
- ½ cup of non-Fat: Greek yogurt
- ¼ cup of mint, finely chopped
- 2 tablespoons of buttermilk
- 1 garlic clove, finely chopped
- 2 pinches of salt

Directions:

1. Select bake mode the set the temperature to preheat the Power XL Air Fryer to 390° F. In a large mixing bowl, addall the meatball ingredients.

2. Roll the meatballs between your hands until it is as small as a golf ball. Place the rolled meatballs into the cooking basket and set the timer for 6 to 8minutes.

3. Meanwhile, combine all the mint yogurt ingredients to a medium mixing bowl, mixing well 4. Garnish the meatballs with fresh mint and olive and enjoy.

Tomato, Cheese 'n Broccoli Quiche

Ready about in: 24 min| Serves 2|

Ingredients

- ½ cup Cheddar Cheese grated
- ½ cup Whole Milk
- 1 Large Carrot, peeled and diced
- 1 Large Tomato, chopped
- 1 small Broccoli, cut into florets
- 1 teaspoons Parsley
- 1 teaspoons Thyme
- 2 Large Eggs
- 2 teaspoons Feta Cheese
- Salt & Pepper

Directions:

1) Lightly grease baking pan of Power XL Air Fryer with cooking spray.

2) Spread carrots, broccoli, and tomato in baking pan.

3) For 10 minutes, cook on 330° F.

4) Meanwhile, in a medium bowl whisk well eggs and milk. Season generously with pepper and salt. Whisk in parsley and thyme.

5) Remove basket and toss the mixture a bit. Sprinkle cheddar cheese. Pour egg mixture over vegetables and cheese.

6) Cook for another 12 minutes or until set to desired doneness.

7) Sprinkle feta cheese and let it sit for 2 minutes.

8) Serve and enjoy.

Tasty Hash Brown

Ready in about 30 mins | Serving 6 | Easy

Ingredients:

- 16 ounces of hash browns
- ¼ cup of olive oil
- ½ teaspoon of paprika
- ½ teaspoon of garlic powder
- Salt and black pepper to the taste
- 1 egg, whisked
- 2 tablespoon of chives, chopped
- 1 cup of cheddar, shredded

Directions:

1. Apply the oil to the Power XL Air Fryer, pump it up to 350° F, and apply brown hash.

2. Remove the paprika, garlic powder, salt, pepper, and egg, mix for 15 minutes, and fry.

3. Add the cheddar and chives, toss, break and serve between plates. Enjoy!

Pork Barbecue Sandwich

Ready in about 1hr 55 min | Servings 4 | Difficult

Ingredients:

- Two slices ofwhite bread
- 1 tbsp of softened butter
- 1/2 lbs of cut pork (in cubes)
- 1 little capsicum
- For sauce barbeque:
- 1/4 tablespoons of Worcestershire
- 1/2 tablespoons of olive oil
- 1/2 crushed garlic flake
- 1/4 cup of onion
- 1/4 tablespoons of powder mustard
- 1/2 tablespoons of sugar
- 1/4 tablespoons of hot chili sauce
- 1 tablespoons of tomatoes ketchup
- 1/2 cup of water.
- A pinch of salt and black chilies to the taste

Directions:

1. Take the bread slices and cut the rims. Now clean the slices in the horizontal way. Heat the sauce ingredients and wait before sauce thickens.

2. Now fill in thepork into the sauce before it gets its flavors. Stir in the capsicum and Peel off skin. The capsicum is sliced into strips. Combine products. And add it to slices of bread.

3. Select bake mode the set the temperature to preheat the Power XL Air Fryer to 300° F for 5 minutes. Open the Fryer basket and put the sandwiches prepared in it so that no 2 Sandwiches bump into each other. Now hold the fryer at 250° F for Fifteen minutes.

4. When the timer reaches 0, then press the cancel button

5. Turn the sandwiches in between the cooking to Cook slices of both.Serve the sandwiches with tomato ketchup or chutney.

Fish Club Sandwich

Ready in about 30 min | Servings 2 | Normal

Ingredients:

- 2 slices of white bread
- 1 tablespoons of softened butter
- 1 tin of tuna
- 1 small capsicum

For Barbeque Sauce:

- ¼ tablespoons of Worcestershire sauce
- ½ tablespoons of olive oil
- ½ flake of garlic crushed
- ¼ cup of chopped onion
- ¼ tablespoons of mustard powder
- ½ tablespoons of sugar
- ¼ tablespoons. of red chili sauce
- 1 tablespoons of tomato ketchup
- ½ cup of water.
- **A pinch of salt and black pepper to taste**

Directions:

1. Take the bread slices and cut the rims. Still cut horizontally on the strips. Heat the sauce ingredients and wait before sauce thickens. Now add the fish to the sauce and whisk before the flavors are acquired.

2. Whisk the capsicum and scrape off the flesh. The capsicum is sliced into strips. Mix the ingredients, and add them to the slices of bread.

3. Preheat the AirFryer to 300° F for 5 minutes. Open the Fryer's basket and put the cooked sandwiches in it, ensuring that no two sandwiches meet each other.

4. Hold the fryer at about 15 minutes now at 250°. Switch the sandwiches to cook both slices in between the cooking process. Serve the strawberry ketchup or mint chutney sandwiches.

Air Fryer Sandwich

Ready in about 16 mins | Serving 2 | Easy

Ingredients:

- 2 English muffins halved
- 2 eggs
- 2 bacon strips
- Salt and black pepper to the taste

Directions:

1. Crack eggs in your Power XL Air Fryer, put bacon on top, cover, and cook at 392° F for 6 minutes.

2. Warm up the English muffin halves in the microwave for a few seconds, split eggs into two halves, place bacon on top, sprinkle salt and pepper, cover with the other two English muffins and serve for breakfast.

Enjoy!

Cheese Sandwich

Ready in about 18 min | Servings 1 | Easy

Ingredients:

- 2 bread slices
- 2 teaspoons of butter
- 2 pieces of cheddar cheese
- A pinch of sweet paprika

Directions:

1. Place the butter on slices of bread, add the cheddar cheese on one, sprinkle the paprika, cover with the other slices of bread, break into 2 halves, put them in the Power XL Air Fryer, and cook for 8 minutes at 370° F, turn them once, put them on a plate and serve.

Enjoy!

Onion Flowers

Ready in about 40 min | Servings 6 | Normal

Ingredients:

- 4 medium-sized onions, peeled

- 4 teaspoons of butter

- 3 teaspoons of vegetable oil

Directions:

1. Cut off the bottom and top of the onions. Cut 4 slits into the onions but not through to the end to make 8 segments.

2. Place the onions in salt water for 4 hours to remove the sharp tang.

3. Heat your Power XL Air Fryer to 356° F.

4. Place the blooming onions in the fryer basket. Add a teaspoon of butter oneach and drizzle with oil—Cook for 30 minutes.

5. Remove the charred outer layer and serve.

Sweet Pepper and Potato Stuffed Bread Rolls

Ready in about 20 min | Servings 3 | Normal

Ingredients:

- 6 medium-sized potatoes, boiled
- 2 teaspoons of flour
- 6 slices of white bread
- 1 tablespoon of sesame seed
- 1 pound of chopped bell peppers (red and green)
- ½ teaspoon of chat masala seasoning
- Salt to taste

Directions:

1. Mash the cooked potatoes in a large bowl and add the seasoning and salt. Stir thoroughly.

2. Add water to the flour to make a thick slurry mixture. Mix sesame seedsand the chopped pepper in a separate bowl.

3. Peel off the brown edges of the bread and use a rolling pin to flatten it. Putthe potato stuffing on the edge of the bread and roll it into a cylinder.

4. Seal the rolls by brushing the edge with the flour mixture. Use the mixtureto coat the rolls as well. Place the rolls in the mixture of pepper and sesameseeds and allow tocoat.

5. Heat your Power XL AirFryer to 330° F and place the rolls in it. Bake for 5 minutes andremove it. Serve hot with ketchup.

Crispy Parsley and Garlic Mushrooms

Ready in about 20 min | Servings 4 | Normal

Ingredients:

- 2 slices of white bread
- 3 teaspoons of finely chopped parsley
- 16 small mushrooms
- 4 teaspoons of melted butter
- 1 clove of garlic, crushed
- ½ teaspoon of black pepper

Directions:

1.Heat your Power XL Air Fryer to 390°F.

2.When the timer reaches 0, then press the cancel button

3. Grind the bread using a food processor into fine crumbs. Add the parsley, garlic, and pepper and mix thoroughly. Add the melted butter and stir.

4. Remove all the mushroom stalks and Put the breadcrumbs into the caps. Press to keep breadcrumbs firm in the cap.

5. Put the caps into the fryer basket and cook for 8 minutes until they becomecrisp and golden brown.

Crispy Broccoli Tots

Ready in about 50 min | Servings 4 | Normal

Ingredients:

- 2 cups of broccoli florets
- 1¼ cup of white cheddar cheese
- 1¼ cup of panko crumbs
- 1/4 cup of parmesan cheese
- 2 eggs, beaten
- 1 teaspoon of kosher salt

Directions:

1.Pulse broccoli with a food processor until finely crumbed.

2. Combine broccoli, cheeses, panko crumbs, and salt in a large bowl. Add eggs and mix thoroughly.

3. Roll mixture into small balls and refrigerate for 30 minutes to firm— Preheat Power XL Air Fryer to 350°F.

4. Place the broccoli tots into the AirFryer and then cook until browned and crispy for 12 minutes. Remove and serve.

Roasted Winter Vegetables

Ready in about 25 min | Servings 6 | Normal

Ingredients:

- 2 red onions, cut into wedges
- 1 1/3 cup of parsnips, peeled and cut into 2 cm cubes
- 1 1/3 cup of butternut squash, halved, seeded, and cubed
- 1 1/3 cup of celery, peeled and cut into2 cm cubes
- 1 tablespoon of fresh thyme needles
- 1tablespoon of olive oil, pepper, and salt

Directions:

1. Select bake mode the set the temperature to preheat the Powwr XL Air Fryer to 390° F.

2. Combine the cut vegetables with the olive oil and thyme and season well to taste.

3. Place the veggies into the basket and place the basket into the Air Fryer.

4. Roast the vegetables for 20 minutes, stirring once until brown and done.

Cheesy Polenta

Ready in about 1hr 5mins | Servings 6 | Difficult

Ingredients:

- 2 ½ cups of cooked polenta
- 1 cup of marinara sauce
- 1/4 cup of parmesan, shaved
- 1 tablespoon of vegetable oil
- Salt to taste

Directions

1. Grease a baking tray with vegetable oil. Place the polenta into the tray and then refrigerate for 1 hour to firm.

2. Select bake mode the set the temperature to preheat the Power XL Air Fryer to 350°F. Remove the tray from the fridge and cut the polenta into equal slices.

3. Place the slices into the Air Fryer and cook minutes until crispy or for 5-6 minutes.

4. Sprinkle with parmesan, season with salt, and serve with marinara on the side.

Cajun Shrimp

Ready in about 10 min | Servings 4 | Normal

Ingredients:

- 1¼ pounds of tiger shrimp
- ¼ teaspoon of smoked paprika
- ½teaspoon of old bay seasoning
- ¼ teaspoon of cayenne pepper
- 1 tablespoon of olive oil
- 1 pinch of salt

Directions:

1. Select bake mode the set the temperature to preheat the Power Xl Air Fryer to 390°F. Combine all ingredients in amixing bowl; let the shrimp coat well with the oil and spices.

2. Place the shrimp into the cooking basket in the Air Fryer and cook for 5 minutes.

3. When the timer reaches 0, then press the cancel button

4.. Serve with rice and enjoy.

Broccoli Rounds with Cheese

Ready in about 2hrs25 min | Servings 6 | Normal

Ingredients

- 16-ounce Broccoli, chopped
- 3 cups of cheddar cheese, shredded
- 3 eggs
- 1 cup of flour
- 1 cup of breadcrumbs
- Salt and pepper to taste

Directions

1. Whisk the eggs in abowl and then add the broccoli, cheese, and flour to make a dough. Cover and then put inside the refrigerator for at least 2 hours.

2. Use a spoonful of the mixture to compress into balls, then roll into the breadcrumbs to coat.

3. Select bake mode the set the temperature to preheat the Power XL Air Fryer to 350° F. Fry the broccoli rounds in batches for 4 to 5 minutes.

4. When the timer reaches 0, then press the cancel button

5. Serve with ranch dip and enjoy.

Coconut Chicken Bites

Ready in about 25 min | Servings 4 | Normal

Ingredients:

- 2 teaspoons of garlic powder
- 2 eggs
- Salt and black pepper to the taste
- ¾ cup of panko bread crumbs
- ¾ cup of coconut, shredded
- Cooking spray
- 8 chicken tenders

Directions:

1. Mix the eggs with salt, pepper, and garlic powder in a cup, then whisk well.

2. Mix coconut and panko in another dish, then mix well.

3. Mix the chicken tenders into the shells and roll one well in the coconut.

4. Sprinkle chicken bits with cooking oil, bring them in the Power Xl Air Fryers bowl, and cook for 10 minutes at 350° F.

5. Put them up on a tray, and act as an appetizer.

Enjoy!

Cauliflower Snack

Ready in about 25 min | Servings 4 | Normal

Ingredients:

- 4 cups of cauliflower florets
- 1 cup of panko bread crumbs
- ¼ cup of butter, melted
- ¼ cup of buffalo sauce
- Mayonnaise for serving

Directions:

1. Mix butter and buffalo sauce in a tub, then shake well.

2. In this combination, roll the cauliflower florets and cover them in crumbs of panko crust.

3. Place these in the basket of your Power XL Air Fryer and cook for 15 minutes at 350° F.

4. Arrange them on a pan, then serve side by side with mayo.

Enjoy!

Sausage Balls

Ready in about 25 min | Servings 9 | Normal

Ingredients:

- 4 ounces of sausage meat, ground
- Salt and black pepper to the taste
- 1 teaspoon of sage
- ½ teaspoon of garlic, minced
- 1 small onion, chopped
- 3 tablespoons of breadcrumbs

Directions:

1. In a bowl, mix sausage with salt, pepper, sage, garlic, onion, and breadcrumbs, stir well and shape small balls out of this mix.

2. Put them in your Power XL Air Fryer's basket, cook at 360° F for 15minutes, divide into bowls

3. When the timer reaches 0, then press the cancel button

4. serve as a snack.

Enjoy!

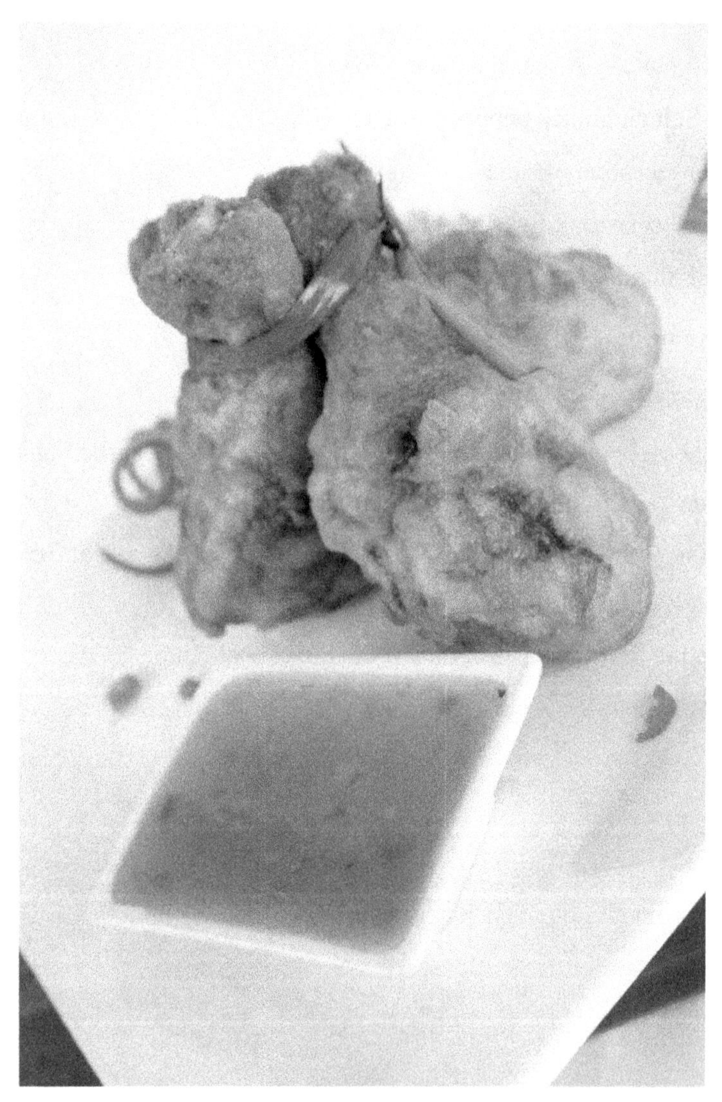

Chicken Dip

Ready in about 35 min | Servings 10 | Normal

Ingredients:

- 3 tablespoons of butter, melted
- 1 cup of yogurt
- 12 ounces of cream cheese
- 2 cups of chicken meat, cooked and shredded
- 2 teaspoons of curry powder
- 4 scallions, chopped
- 6 ounces of Monterey jack cheese, grated
- 1/3 cup of raisins
- ¼ cup of cilantro, chopped
- ½ cup of almonds, sliced
- Salt and black pepper to the taste
- ½ cup of chutney

Directions:

1. In a bowl, mix cream cheese with yogurt and whisk using yourmixer.

2. Add curry powder, scallions, chicken meat, raisins, cheese,cilantro, salt, and pepper and stir everything.

3. Spread this into a baking dish that fist your Power XL Air Fryer, sprink lealmonds on top, place in your Air Fryer, bake at 300° for 25minutes, divide into bowls, top with chutney, and serve as anappetizer.

Enjoy!

Sweet Popcorn

Ready in about 25 min | Servings 4 | Normal

Ingredients:

- 2 tablespoons of corn kernels
- 2 and ½ tablespoons of butter
- 2 ounces of brown sugar

Directions:

1. Place the corn kernels in the pan of your Power XL Air Fryer, cook them for 6 minutes at 400° F, move them to a plate, spread them out, and set them aside for now.

2. Heat a casserole over low pressure, add butter, melt it, add sugar, and whisk before dissolving.

3. Attach popcorn, throw to cover, heat off and scatter over the tray again.

4. Refrigerate, break into bowls, and serve as a snack.

Enjoy!

Squash Fritters

Ready in about 17 min | Servings 4 | Easy

Ingredients:

- 3 ounces of cream cheese
- 1 egg, whisked
- ½ teaspoon of oregano, dried
- A pinch of salt and black pepper
- 1 yellow summer squash, grated
- 1/3 cup of carrot, grated
- 2/3 cup of bread crumbs
- 2 tablespoons of olive oil

Directions:

1. In a bowl, mix cream cheese with salt, pepper, oregano, egg, breadcrumbs, carrot, and squash and stir well.

2. Shape medium patties out of this mix and brush them with the oil.

3. Place squash patties in your Power XL Air Fryer and cook them at 400° F for 7 minutes.

4. When the timer reaches 0, then press the cancel button

5. Serve them

Enjoy!

Cauliflower Buffalo

Ready in about 15 min | Servings 2 | Normal

Ingredients

- 4 cups of cauliflower florets
- 2 spoonful of salted butter, melted
- 1/2 (1-ounce) package of fresh ranch seasoning
- 1/4 cup of buffalo sauce

Directions:

1. Sprinkle the cauliflower with butter in a wide bowl and dry. Put the basket into the Power XL Air Fryer.

2. Adjust the temperature and set the timer to 400° F For 5 minutes.

3. When preparing, shake the basket 2 or 3 times. Drop cauliflower from the fryer basket when tender and sprinkle with buffalo sauce. Serve hot.

Fries Avocado

Ready in about 15 min | Servings 2 | Normal

Ingredients

- 2 Medium advocates
- 1 ounce of pork rinds, finely soiled

Directions:

1. Cut out half of each avocado. Have the pit removed and cut the flesh into 1/4"-thick slices.

2. In a medium bowl, place the pork rinds and press each slice of avocado coated in the pork rinds. Place the pieces of avocado in the Power Xl Air Fryer basket.

3.Change the temperature to 350° F and timer configuration to 5 minutes.

4. Immediately serve.

Coco Milk and Paprika Drumstick

Ready about in**:** 30 min| Serves 6|

Ingredients

- ½ cup almond flour
- ½ cup coconut milk
- ½ teaspoon oregano
- ½ teaspoon paprika
- ½ teaspoon salt
- 3 tablespoons melted butter
- 6 chicken drumsticks

Instructions

1. Select bake mode the set the temperature to Preheat the Power XL Air Fryer for 5 minutes.

2. Soak the chicken drumsticks in coconut milk.

3. In a mixing bowl, combine the almond flour, salt, paprika, and oregano.

4. Dredge the chicken in the almond flour mixture.

5. Place the chicken pieces in the air fryer basket.

6. Air Fry for 30 minutes at 325° F.

7. Halfway through the Cooking Time, give the fryer basket a shape.

8. Drizzle with melted butter once cooked.

PUBLISHIG HOUSE

KULTURE KITCHEN